LAYERS OF LEARNING
YEAR FOUR • UNIT NINETEEN

TECHNOLOGY
HOME STATE STUDY II
HABITATS
ARCHITECTURE

Published by HooDoo Publishing
United States of America
© 2017 Layers of Learning
Copies of maps or activities may be made for a particular family or classroom. All other
rights reserved. Printed in the United States of America.
(Grilled Cheese BTN Font) © Fontdiner - www.fontdiner.com
ISBN #978-1974219612

Units at a Glance: Topics For All Four Years of the Layers of Learning Program

1	History	Geography	Science	The Arts
1	Mesopotamia	Maps & Globes	Planets	Cave Paintings
2	Egypt	Map Keys	Stars	Egyptian Art
3	Europe	Global Grids	Earth & Moon	Crafts
4	Ancient Greece	Wonders	Satellites	Greek Art
5	Babylon	Mapping People	Humans in Space	Poetry
6	The Levant	Physical Earth	Laws of Motion	List Poems
7	Phoenicians	Oceans	Motion	Moral Stories
8	Assyrians	Deserts	Fluids	Rhythm
9	Persians	Arctic	Waves	Melody
10	Ancient China	Forests	Machines	Chinese Art
11	Early Japan	Mountains	States of Matter	Line & Shape
12	Arabia	Rivers & Lakes	Atoms	Color & Value
13	Ancient India	Grasslands	Elements	Texture & Form
14	Ancient Africa	Africa	Bonding	African Tales
15	First North Americans	North America	Salts	Creative Kids
16	Ancient South America	South America	Plants	South American Art
17	Celts	Europe	Flowering Plants	Jewelry
18	Roman Republic	Asia	Trees	Roman Art
19	Christianity	Australia & Oceania	Simple Plants	Instruments
20	Roman Empire	You Explore	Fungi	Composing Music

2	History	Geography	Science	The Arts
1	Byzantines	Turkey	Climate & Seasons	Byzantine Art
2	Barbarians	Ireland	Forecasting	Illumination
3	Islam	Arabian Peninsula	Clouds & Precipitation	Creative Kids
4	Vikings	Norway	Special Effects	Viking Art
5	Anglo Saxons	Britain	Wild Weather	King Arthur Tales
6	Charlemagne	France	Cells & DNA	Carolingian Art
7	Normans	Nigeria	Skeletons	Canterbury Tales
8	Feudal System	Germany	Muscles, Skin, Cardio	Gothic Art
9	Crusades	Balkans	Digestive & Senses	Religious Art
10	Burgundy, Venice, Spain	Switzerland	Nerves	Oil Paints
11	Wars of the Roses	Russia	Health	Minstrels & Plays
12	Eastern Europe	Hungary	Metals	Printmaking
13	African Kingdoms	Mali	Carbon Chemistry	Textiles
14	Asian Kingdoms	Southeast Asia	Non-metals	Vivid Language
15	Mongols	Caucasus	Gases	Fun With Poetry
16	Medieval China & Japan	China	Electricity	Asian Arts
17	Pacific Peoples	Micronesia	Circuits	Arts of the Islands
18	American Peoples	Canada	Technology	Indian Legends
19	The Renaissance	Italy	Magnetism	Renaissance Art I
20	Explorers	Caribbean Sea	Motors	Renaissance Art II

www.Layers-of-Learning.com

3	History	Geography	Science	The Arts
1	Age of Exploration	Argentina & Chile	Classification & Insects	Fairy Tales
2	The Ottoman Empire	Egypt & Libya	Reptiles & Amphibians	Poetry
3	Mogul Empire	Pakistan & Afghanistan	Fish	Mogul Arts
4	Reformation	Angola & Zambia	Birds	Reformation Art
5	Renaissance England	Tanzania & Kenya	Mammals & Primates	Shakespeare
6	Thirty Years' War	Spain	Sound	Baroque Music
7	The Dutch	Netherlands	Light & Optics	Baroque Art I
8	France	Indonesia	Bending Light	Baroque Art II
9	The Enlightenment	Korean Peninsula	Color	Art Journaling
10	Russia & Prussia	Central Asia	History of Science	Watercolors
11	Conquistadors	Baltic States	Igneous Rocks	Creative Kids
12	Settlers	Peru & Bolivia	Sedimentary Rocks	Native American Art
13	13 Colonies	Central America	Metamorphic Rocks	Settler Sayings
14	Slave Trade	Brazil	Gems & Minerals	Colonial Art
15	The South Pacific	Australasia	Fossils	Principles of Art
16	The British in India	India	Chemical Reactions	Classical Music
17	The Boston Tea Party	Japan	Reversible Reactions	Folk Music
18	Founding Fathers	Iran	Compounds & Solutions	Rococo
19	Declaring Independence	Samoa & Tonga	Oxidation & Reduction	Creative Crafts I
20	The American Revolution	South Africa	Acids & Bases	Creative Crafts II

4	History	Geography	Science	The Arts
1	American Government	USA	Heat & Temperature	Patriotic Music
2	Expanding Nation	Pacific States	Motors & Engines	Tall Tales
3	Industrial Revolution	U.S. Landscapes	Energy	Romantic Art I
4	Revolutions	Mountain West States	Energy Sources	Romantic Art II
5	Africa	U.S. Political Maps	Energy Conversion	Impressionism I
6	The West	Southwest States	Earth Structure	Impressionism II
7	Civil War	National Parks	Plate Tectonics	Post Impressionism
8	World War I	Plains States	Earthquakes	Expressionism
9	Totalitarianism	U.S. Economics	Volcanoes	Abstract Art
10	Great Depression	Heartland States	Mountain Building	Kinds of Art
11	World War II	Symbols & Landmarks	Chemistry of Air & Water	War Art
12	Modern East Asia	The South	Food Chemistry	Modern Art
13	India's Independence	People of America	Industry	Pop Art
14	Israel	Appalachian States	Chemistry of Farming	Modern Music
15	Cold War	U.S. Territories	Chemistry of Medicine	Free Verse
16	Vietnam War	Atlantic States	Food Chains	Photography
17	Latin America	New England States	Animal Groups	Latin American Art
18	Civil Rights	Home State Study I	Instincts	Theater & Film
19	Technology	Home State Study II	Habitats	Architecture
20	Terrorism	America in Review	Conservation	Creative Kids

Unit 4-19

Printable Pack

This unit includes printables at the end. To make life easier for you we also created digital printable packs for each unit. To retrieve your printable pack for Unit 4-19, please visit

www.layers-of-learning.com/digital-printable-packs/

Put the printable pack in your shopping cart and use this coupon code:

724UNIT4-19

Your printable pack will be free.

Layers of Learning Introduction

This is part of a series of units in the Layers of Learning homeschool curriculum, including the subjects of history, geography, science, and the arts. Children from 1st through 12th can participate in the same curriculum at the same time - family school style.

The units are intended to be used in order as the basis of a complete curriculum (once you add in a systematic math, reading, and writing program). You begin with Year 1 Unit 1 no matter what ages your children are. Spend about 2 weeks on each unit. You pick and choose the activities within the unit that appeal to you and read the books from the book list that are available to you or find others on the same topic from your library. We highly recommend that you use the timeline in every history section as the backbone. Then flesh out your learning with reading and activities that highlight the topics you think are the most important.

Alternatively, you can use the units as activity ideas to supplement another curriculum in any order you wish. You can still use them with all ages of children at the same time.

When you've finished with Year One, move on to Year Two, Year Three, and Year Four. Then begin again with Year One and work your way through the years again. Now your children will be older, reading more involved books, and writing more in depth. When you have completed the sequence for the second time, you start again on it for the third and final time. If your student began with Layers of Learning in 1st grade and stayed with it all the way through she would go through the four year rotation three times, firmly cementing the information in her mind in ever increasing depth. At each level you should expect increasing amounts of outside reading and writing. High schoolers in particular should be reading extensively, and if possible, participating in discussion groups.

These icons will guide you in spotting activities and books that are appropriate for the age of child you are working with. But if you think an activity is too juvenile or too difficult for your kids, adjust accordingly. The icons are not there as rules, just guides.

> ☺ 1st-4th
> ☻ 5th-8th
> ☻ 9th-12th

Within each unit we share:

EXPLORATIONS, activities relating to the topic;
EXPERIMENTS, usually associated with science topics;
EXPEDITIONS, field trips;
EXPLANATIONS, teacher helps or educational philosophies.

In the sidebars we also include Additional Layers, Famous Folks, Fabulous Facts, On the Web, and other extra related topics that can take you off on tangents, exploring the world and your interests with a bit more freedom. The curriculum will always be there to pull you back on track when you're ready.

UNIT NINETEEN
TECHNOLOGY - HOME STATE STUDY II - HABITATS - ARCHITECTURE

Being the richest man in the cemetery doesn't matter to me. Going to bed at night saying we've done something wonderful, that's what matters to me.
-Steve Jobs

LIBRARY LIST

HISTORY

Search for: technology, history of technology, information revolution, inventions, airplane, medicine, computer, plastic, petroleum, farming, industry, Einstein, Tesla, Alexander Graham Bell, Robert Goddard, Henry Ford, Wright Brothers, Thomas Edison

☺ ☺ ☻ Technology by Roger Bridgman from DK Eyewitness.

☻ You Wouldn't Want to Live Without Cell Phones by Jim Pipe. Talks a bit about the invention of phones.

☺ ☻ 100 Inventions That Made History from DK.

☺ ☻ Great Inventors and Inventions by Bruce LeFontaine. A Dover coloring book.

☺ ☻ An Illustrated Timeline of Inventions and Inventors by Kremena T. Spengler.

☺ ☻ The Story of Inventions by Anna Claybourne.

☺ ☻ Technology: A Byte-Sized World by Simon Basher. How technology works.

☺ ☻ 100 Scientists Who Shaped World History by John Tiner.

☻ Technology by Clive Gifford. How technology works and what's out there.

☻ The Wright Brothers: How They Invented the Airplane by Russell Freedman.

☺ ☻ Steve Jobs: Insanely Great by Jessie Hartland. A graphic biography of one of the most influential inventors of the last 50 years.

☻ Science and Technology in World History by James E. McClellan and Harold Dorn. Covers the whole scope of world history in less than 500 pages. Well-written.

☻ Where Wizards Stay Up Late: The Origins Of The Internet by Katie Hafner. Written in the late 90s, so it's a bit dated, but excellent look at one of the greatest inventions of mankind and how it came about. Entertaining and well-written.

☻ The Wright Brothers by David McCullough.

☻ The Battery: How Portable Power Sparked a Technological Revolution by Henry Schlesinger. About the history of electricity and how it has changed the world.

☻ A Mind at Play: How Claude Shannon Invented the Information Age by Jimmy Soni. This is the guy who realized that all information, sound, images, text, is really data. Without him computers would never have been anything but glorified calculators.

GEOGRAPHY	Search for: Your home state, novels set in your home state. Often local libraries will have a special section filled with books and resources about the state they are located in, so make sure to ask. Also see the library list for Unit 4-18 for book suggestions.
SCIENCE	Search for: habitat, biome, niche ☺ The ABCs of Habitats by Bobbie Kalman. ☺ I See a Kookaburra!: Discovering Animal Habitats Around the World by Steve Jenkins and Robin Page. ☺ A Rainforest Habitat by Molly Aloian and Bobbie Kalman. Part of a series. ☺ Nature's Patchwork Quilt: Understanding Habitats by Mary Miche. ☺ About Habitats: Mountains by Cathryn and John Sill. Part of a series. ☺ ☻ Draw, Write, Now Book 6: Animals Habitats by Marie Hablitzel and Kim Stitzer. ☺ ☻ The Wonder Garden: Wander Through 5 Habitats to Discover 80 Amazing Animals by Jenny Broom. Information is limited, but uses scientific names of animals and captivating illustrations. Good springboard for talking about habitats. ☺ ☻ A Journey Into an Estuary by Rebecca L. Johnson. Part of the "Biomes of North America" series. Look for others. ☻ Amazing Biome Projects You Can Build Yourself by Donna Latham. A project book, but filled with lots of information as well. ☺ ☻ Ecology by Stephen Pollock from DK Eyewitness.
THE ARTS	Search for: architecture, famous buildings, homes, cathedrals, castles, names of specific buildings. ☺ ☻ ☻ Lego Architecture kits are Lego block kits you use to make famous buildings and skylines from around the world. Find them in toy stores or on Amazon. ☺ ☻ ☻ Built To Last by David Macaulay. Highly recommended. Also search for single titles like Castle, City, Mosque, and Pyramid by the same author. ☺ From Mud Huts to Skyscrapers: Architecture for Children by Christine Paxmann. ☺ Look at that Building!: A First Book of Structures by Scott Ritchie. ☺ ☻ The Story of Buildings: From the Pyramids to the Sydney Opera House and Beyond by Patrick Dillon and Stephen Biesty. ☺ ☻ Architecture: Cool Women Who Design Structures by Elizabeth Schmermund and Lena Chandhok. From the *Girls in Science* series. ☺ ☻ Architecture Explained by Neil Stevenson. ☺ ☻ The Visual Dictionary of Buildings by DK. ☺ ☻ Grand Constructions by Gian Paolo Ceserani.

HISTORY: TECHNOLOGY

If you could look back at the world as it was in 1800, it would be almost unrecognizable to modern eyes. Long distance com- munication was slow and expensive, travel was long and arduous, and most people had to farm to feed the few who lived in cities as well as themselves. People regularly died of what we now consid- er to be mild diseases or injuries, and women had to labor long hours to care for and provide the basic necessities of their fam- ilies. By 1900 people were moving to cities in droves. The new machines of the Industrial Revolution had made farming easier and there was work in factories.

Since then, our lives have been transformed by things like air- planes, rockets, the assembly line, fertilizers, plastics, and wash- ing machines. All these new inventions radically transformed the way people live their daily lives and the way society functioned as a whole. Consumerism, growing wealth, a large middle class, and dependence on society for daily life are hallmarks of the world now.

April 8, 1958

F. G. LUDWIG
ROLLER BOARD DEVICE

2,829,891

Filed June 8, 1955

2 Sheets—Sheet 1

Fig.1

This is a patent drawing from 1958 for a toy called a balance board. Pat- ents, or the legal ability for an inventor to claim the rights to his invention, are essential for progress. People, it turns out, don't work for nothing.

☺ ☺ ☺ EXPLORATION: Timeline

This timeline covers some of the most important technological advances since 1900. You can, of course, add more inventions to the timeline. You will find printable timeline squares at the end of this unit. Place the timeline squares on a wall timeline or in a notebook timeline.

☺ ☺ EXPLORATION: The Airplane

Wilbur and Orville Wright invented the airplane, a heavier-than-air machine that could carry a human being and be steered in the air. Their first successful flight was in 1903 at Kitty Hawk, North Carolina in the United States. With others, they worked to perfect the techniques that would keep an airplane in the air. Within ten years planes were being flown for travel, as mobile observation posts, for mail delivery, and as weapons.

The significant thing about the airplane is that it created a whole new way for humans to move about. People could now fly. Since you've grown up with it, you may not fully appreciate the significance of that. People can fly. Beyond the sheer miraculous nature of flight, the rapid travel that airplanes created shrunk the world and made travel, trade, and communication fast and inexpensive.

Make an airplane model out of craft sticks and hot glue.

What are airplanes used for today? Write up a list on a long, narrow slip of paper and attach it to the back of your plane, like a banner.

Additional Layer

The story of the airplane only begins with the Wrights. Watch "Boeing: A Century of Aviation from the Wright Brothers to Mars" to learn about the development afterward. https://youtu.be/DQ9dWacQdPw

Famous Folks

Hermann Staudinger was a German organic chemist who demonstrated that macromolecules, aka polymers, exist. He won a Nobel prize for his work in 1953.

Baekeland accidentally created the world's first plastic, but Staudinger understood how polymers worked and opened the way to the development of thousands of applications.

Fabulous Fact

About 80% of air is nitrogen, but it is much more rare in the earth. Animals and plants cannot use atmospheric nitrogen. Before Haber, the only way to move nitrogen from the air to the soil was with nitrogen fixing bacteria. It was a severely limiting factor to plant life, especially in terms of crops.

☺ ☺ ☺ EXPLORATION: Plastics

Bakelite was the first plastic made from synthetic components and used to produce commercial products. It was invented in 1907 by Leo Baekeland in Yonkers, New York. It was used to make everything from children's toys to telephones to insulating components for electricity. Since then, dozens of forms of plastics have been invented including vinyl, polyethylene, polypropylene, polyvinyl chloride, nylon, polyester, polycarbonate, acrylonitrile butadiene styrene, and silicone, plus many more.

Plastics are lightweight, strong, easily molded into any shape, non-porous, and easy to produce. They also act as insulators to electricity because they are non-conductive. These properties have made plastics essential to modern life. There is almost nothing you do that doesn't involve plastics in some way. The modern medical industry relies on plastics, as does manufacturing, travel, communications, computers, electricity, and agriculture.

Look around your home and find things that are *not* made of plastic or with plastic components. It will be a lot tougher than finding things that are. Even fabrics and flooring and wall paper are made of polyesters, polyester blends, or vinyl, all forms of plastic. My wood floors are coated with polyurethane, a plastic.

Choose eight plastic items and do a little research to find out what kind of plastic each of them is made of. At the end of this unit you will find an "8 Ways We Use _____" printable. Cut out the title and glue it to another piece of paper. Write "Plastics" in the space on the title. Then cut out the large rectangle. Cut along the dashed lines. Glue the center of the rectangle to the piece of paper beneath the title. This will create 8 flaps. On top of each flap, draw a picture of your plastic item. Under the flap tell what type of plastic it is and a few features of that plastic.

☺ ☺ ☺ EXPLORATION: Synthetic Fertilizer

In 1909, a German scientist named Fritz Haber figured out how to take nitrogen from the air and convert it into liquid ammonia. The technology was first used in making explosives for the German war effort of World War I, but it was soon converted into synthetic fertilizers.

Today 450 million tons of nitrogen fertilizer are produced each year using the Haber process. These fertilizers have quadrupled the productivity of farm land. If farm yields had remained what they were per acre in 1900, today we would require nearly half of all ice-free land for agriculture instead of the 15% we now use. It is estimated that of the world's 7 billion people, a little more than

5 billion of them depend on the Haber process for their existence. Their ancestors would have starved to death or never been born without the increase in productivity. Technology often lifts what we think are the limits of human and earth capabilities.

Freehand draw a map of the world on a piece of paper. Color in about 15% of the land with light green to show the amount of land used for agriculture. Then add dark green until about half the land is colored in, showing how much would be needed if the Haber process hadn't been invented.

Finally, draw a graph showing the world population since 1900. Use the data in the chart. Note also that the population of the world in 1800 was 1 billion. It took one hundred years to add .6 billion people. In the next hundred years another 6 billion would be added. Almost all of this growth is because of the Haber process and pesticides.

Year	Population in billions
1900	1.6
1927	2
1960	3
1974	4
1987	5
1999	6
2011	7

Haber Process

Land needed to feed the world
Land needed if Haber process had not been invented

Synthetic fertilizers first are used widely

GREEN REVOLUTION
Over a billion people saved from starvation due to fertilizers and pesticides

1.6 billion, 3 billion, 4 billion, 5 billion, 6 billion, 7 billion

Haber process invented.

1900   1950   2000

Haber Process enabled Population Growth

Additional Layer

Air conditioning is another invention that almost made our main list. It may not seem that significant, unless you realize that none of the hot places of the world would have much business or industry without it. Houston or Singapore without air conditioning? I don't think so.

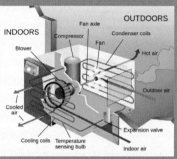

Photo by Pbroks13, CC by 3.0, Wikimedia

Additional Layer

The Green Revolution was a set of initiatives that spread fertilizers, pesticides, and new high yield breeds of plants throughout the world, especially to poorer countries. Most people believe that without the Green Revolution, over a billion people would have died of famine in the 20th century.

The leader of this movement was a scientist named Norman Borlaug. He received the Nobel Peace Prize in 1970.

Famous Folks

When we were kids, schools in the U.S. taught that Henry Ford invented the automobile. While that isn't true, it is true that he invented the affordable automobile. Learn more about Henry Ford and his life.

Additional Layer

Ford's real achievement was to increase efficiency many times over. He thought about every aspect of the job and broke it down, simplified it, and made it as efficient as possible.

Shortly after, a new field of efficiency was developed. The leading efficiency experts were Lilian and Frank Gilbreth.

Their story is told in the fascinating novel, *Cheaper by the Dozen*, which was written by two of their children.

☺ ☺ ☺ EXPLORATION: The Assembly Line

The assembly line was perfected at the Ford factory in the early 1900s. It allowed a process that would take weeks for one individual to be done in just hours. This affected society in several ways. First, goods produced on an assembly line could be made much more cheaply so people could afford them, creating a consumer culture. Second, it meant the economy switched from a base of craftsmen to a base of factory workers. Third, it meant that a single individual no longer knew how to make any complete product at all. Today parts are made all over the world and then gathered for final assembly. Almost no one knows how to take any one item from raw materials to a finished product anymore. Finally, the assembly line increased production and profits so much that wages rose and working hours dropped. It was the assembly line that made Saturdays at the beach possible.

Assembly lines used conveyor belts to move the product along a line of workers who stood still. The workers would do one specific task as each product came past their station. Make a model conveyor belt and then write on it what the assembly line did to change society.

To make a convey or belt you will need a box, like a milk box, a couple of dowel sticks or pencils, and some paper.

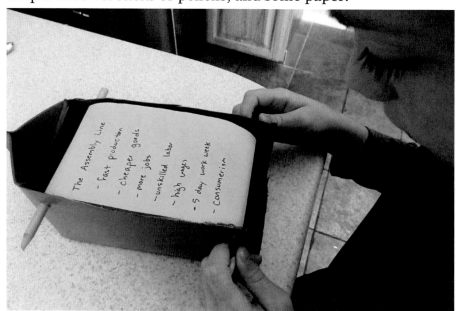

Cut one side off of the box. Punch holes through the box from one side to the other just large enough to slide your dowels through. Trim paper down to fit inside your box and make a loop of paper to go around your dowels. Before you install your paper, write things you think changed in society because of the invention of the assembly line.

☺ ☺ ☺ EXPEDITION: Factory

Find out if there is a factory or plant near you that allows tours. Before you go, learn more about factories, assembly lines, interchangeable parts, and the specific industry you'll be touring. Have a few good questions ready to ask your tour guide about the factory. When you come home, write what you have learned.

☺ ☺ ☺ EXPLORATION: Penicillin

Penicillin was discovered in 1928 by Scottish physician Alexander Fleming. It began to be used to treat illness in 1942. Before that time, illnesses caused by bacteria couldn't be treated directly. You had to just let the disease run its course and hope the body could fight it off. After the breakthrough discovery of something that could fight bacterial diseases, dozens of other antibiotic drugs were developed.

Things that used to mean death, like tuberculosis and syphilis, have been nearly eradicated or are easily treated in the developed world. People who have surgery hardly ever die from infections now, but bacteria used to kill most surgery patients. Often surgery is avoided entirely because of antibiotics, particularly amputations due to infected limbs. Women used to frequently die from infections contracted during childbirth, but we no longer fear for the lives of mothers the way we used to. The processes and technologies used to produce penicillin are now used in the development of cancer drugs and autoimmune disease treatments.

Penicillin was first cultured, along with bacteria, in petri dishes in Fleming's lab. For this activity you are going to make five circles, like petri dishes. In each circle draw a sketch of one of the people who helped develop the penicillin drug. We used these:

The development of Penicillin

- Alexander Fleming - discovered penicillin
- Howard Florey - developed the drug with an Oxford team
- Ernst Chain - teamed with Florey to develop the drug
- Andrew J. Moyer - and the USDA lab learned to mass produce penicillin
- Dorothy Hodgkin - isolated the structure of

Additional Layer

There was a huge push during World War II to develop commercially viable ways to mass produce penicillin. Saving soldiers' lives and limbs was a top priority for the U.S. and Britain during the war, so they funneled funding and scientists into the project. Without the war more people would have died of disease than died in the fighting.

Wars of the 20th century were huge catalysts for invention. Learn what else was invented or developed because of the World Wars.

Additional Layer

The other day Harrison crashed hard on his bike. His elbow and knee were both scraped up pretty badly. A wound like that could easily become infected. In fact, people used to die from simple scrapes and cuts that became infected. We used an antibiotic cream on the wound, something that wouldn't have been possible before the 1950s.

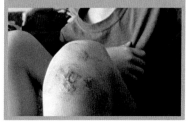

Fabulous Fact

Access to electricity for household and business use is a hallmark of development. Places in the world without a developed electric grid will not be able to catch up economically or socially until they have it. It is probably only equal to education in its power to better the well-being of the world. About 1.3 billion people are still without electricity in the world.

Additional Layer

Our modern world is utterly dependent on electricity and other forms of energy. In fact, if the electric grid were to fail for more than a few days it would be a disaster unlike any seen on the face of the world. People would die by the millions.

Think about that and then think about all the things we rely on electricity to do for us. Could you get food, prepare food, wash your clothes or your body, do your work, or enjoy leisure time without electricity?

penicillin, which made synthetic antibiotics possible

Cut out the circles and then glue the circles to another piece of paper. Give the paper a title and decorate it. We also added a quote from Fleming: "The more complex the world becomes, the more difficult it is to complete something without cooperation with others."

☺ ☺ ☺ EXPLORATION: Electrification

Electricity was discovered in the late 1700s, but it wasn't really put to use until the 20th century. By 1930 most homes in North America and Europe were powered by electricity, and all of the factories were. Electrification is using electricity to power homes, offices, and factories. Electrification made people more efficient and fueled the technology that followed. There is a strong correlation between the upswing in wealth and the output of new technologies with the widespread use of electricity that occurred between 1920 and 1950.

Draw a light bulb shape on a piece of paper. Fold the paper in half first and draw just one half, then cut it out while still folded to make a symmetrical design. Place your cutout light bulb on another sheet of paper. Trace around the light bulb with chalk or oil pastels, then use a cotton ball or flat paint brush to smear the chalk away from the light bulb. Spray clear craft fixative on the project, and let it dry. Write some of the differences electrification has made in the world inside the light bulb.

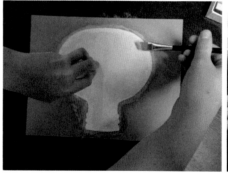 

☺ EXPLORATION: The Black Box

Before the 1930s we knew that organisms were made up of cells, and we knew that cells had nuclei and the Golgi apparatus, but we didn't know much more. The rest of the parts of the cell were so tiny that they couldn't be seen, and the processes they went through were so complicated that we couldn't begin to understand what was really happening. The cell was a black box, so to speak. We knew it was there, we knew there were things inside it, but we didn't know what they were or how they worked.

After the invention of the electron microscope by Ernst Ruska in 1933, all of that changed. Things at a sub-cellular level, including DNA, could now be seen, and what can be seen can be experimented on and analyzed. The understanding of the functions of a cell have created an explosion in medical knowledge and technology.

Besides seeing inside of cells, scientists were able to see viruses for the first time. They were able to study their structure and functions which, in turn, has led to the development of medicines that can fight viral diseases much more effectively than ever before.

Electron microscopes work by bombarding the specimen with electrons. When the electrons bounce off, a picture is recorded and formed. You can try out a virtual electron microscope here: http://school.discoveryeducation.com/lessonplans/interact/vemwindow.html.

Make a box out of black paper. You can use the printable from the end of this unit. Cut on the solid lines, fold on the dashed lines. Glue the tabs. Glue a drawing of a cell inside the bottom of the box. Inside the lid of the box, glue a piece of paper with a paragraph about how the electron microscope revealed the inside of cells and led to new medical knowledge.

 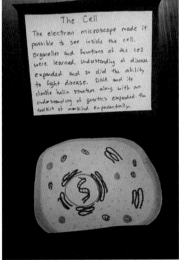

☺ ☺ ☺ **EXPLORATION: Washing Machine**
The automatic washing machine was invented in 1937. It was soon followed by other labor saving household appliances from handheld mixers to vacuum cleaners and dishwashers. As innocuous as these appliances sound, they completely changed society. Women, half the population of the world, no longer had to work long hours of difficult labor to keep their households in order.

Fabulous Fact

Ribosomes were discovered in the 1950s by George Emil Palade, a Romanian scientist, using the electron microscope.

There are several diseases that are caused by ribosomal abnormalities. In addition, ribosome abnormalities have been linked to some cancers, and harnessing the power of ribosomes is used as a tumor suppressant. None of this would have been possible without the electron microscope.

Fabulous Fact

"Black box" is a concept in science and engineering to indicate that you can see the box and what goes in and what comes out, but the things that happen inside are a complete mystery.

Fabulous Fact

Though washing machines were invented in 1937, production and advances in design were halted during WWII so factories could make war materials. Washing machines didn't really become household items until around 1950. They were more expensive than they are now, but demand was still high.

Writer's Workshop

The washing machine is the one household appliance that I could absolutely not live without. When we have a power outage I cook on our wood stove, wash dishes with water heated on the stove, flush toilets with melted snow water, and sweep instead of vacuum. But the dirty clothes just pile up until the power comes back on.

What do you miss most when the power goes out? Write about it in your writer's notebook.

Additional Layer

The modern world can be hard on the natural world. We produce enormous amounts of garbage and use far more resources than ever before in the history of the world. We're still learning how to control our consumption, recycle our waste, and keep our planet clean. Someday, no doubt, our descendants will be horrified at what slobs we all were.

They were free to do other things while still having a family. It took a few decades for the culture to catch up, but before long women were in the workforce, doing the same jobs as men. This radically changed society in untold ways, having an affect on the family, the labor force, the economy, and politics. It also meant women had leisure time to read, to think, to learn, and to have hobbies. Having household appliances is like having a house full of servants to do the work for you, only much less expensive and of course, no one has to be the servant.

Get a tub or sink of soapy water and try washing a few items of clothing by hand. You have to really scrub, rubbing the cloth against itself to get it clean. Then rinse it in water as hot as you can stand. Ring it out by hand. Dry it outside on a line. Now imagine doing that for all of your household's clothing and bedding. Every week. For the rest of your life.

Craft or paint a piece of paper to look like the front of a front loading washing machine. On the back, or inside the door (you can leave a flap) write information about the invention of the washing machine and how it changed the lives of women and families.

☺ ☺ ☺ EXPLORATION: Integrated Circuit

The integrated circuit is the technology that all modern computers are based on, whether they are in the front panel of your fridge, in your smartphone, or inside your car. It is the set of electronic circuits that are on a flat panel or chip made of a semiconductor. Integrated circuits are the building block of everything we call "tech." The IC was invented by Jack Kilby in 1958. Since then, there have been new improvements in their technology every year, making the chips more powerful, smaller, and cheaper.

We use integrated circuits in almost every aspect of our lives. Our clothes, toys, tools, and gadgets are built in factories with chips. We communicate on devices that use chips. We research and learn and create with technology. Medicine, business, and even our trucks and trains use integrated circuits.

Use Prezi, free online presentation software, to create a report or presentation about the integrated circuit and how it has impacted modern life. Choose 5-6 ways the integrated circuit is used and explain how that has expanded human capabilities and efficiency.

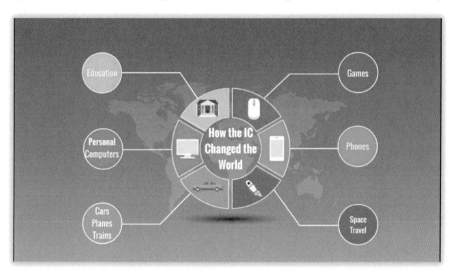

☺ ☻ **EXPLORATION: The Impact of the Internet**
The Internet changed everything. In 1990, people studied, worked, played, and communicated much differently than they do today. The world felt larger and more remote. Talk with someone older, like your parent or grandparent, who remembers what it was like before everyone had a computer and the internet. Ask them if they remember getting their first computer and what they did with it. Ask them if they remember when they first learned to use e-mail or a search engine. Ask them how they found information for a school report or someone's phone number. How did they navigate in their car?

Imagine you have no email, no cell phone, no search engine, no social networks, no online shopping, and no online games. What do you do all day without Netflix, your smart phone, or your electronic games? Spend an entire day with the tech turned off. Then write about what you did without all of your gadgets.

Additional Layer

The creators of integrated circuits, the designers, like to leave their mark, so they often add "graffiti" to the chips when they produce them. These little images or words can only be seen through a microscope. The Smithsonian has photographed a collection of them, which you can see here: http://smithsonianchips.si.edu/chipfun/graff.htm

On the Web

"History of Integrated Circuits: The Foundation of Modern Society" is a YouTube video that explains the history of the IC and how important it is. https://youtu.be/UberD_Pc-O8

Famous Folks

Tim Berners Lee invented the web in 1989 while working for CERN (European Organization for Nuclear Research).

GEOGRAPHY: HOME STATE STUDY II

Teaching Tip

Along with learning about your own state, it can be helpful to look at your region as well. Learn which states border your own and find out what they have in common with each other. Are there things that make your region unique? If you had to describe where you live, what would you say?

Memorization Station

Memorize the population of your city and state, as well as the names of the largest cities and the capital city of your state.

Additional Layer

Make a HOME craft using your state's silhouette. Paint the letters to spell home, replacing the O with the outline of your state. You can do this on a sheet of paper, a canvas, a tile, or a piece of wood. Paint a tiny heart in the spot within your state that you call home.

We started learning about your home state in Unit 4-18. We'll continue on in this unit. This time we'll focus more on the economics, natural resources, and government of your state.

😊 😊 😊 EXPLORATION: Big State Map Continued

Get your big map you worked on from the last unit and add to it. Last time we added on the largest cities, the state capital, major highways, mountains, lakes, rivers, and other features and labeled them all.

First, mark the location of National Parks, State Parks, and landmarks. Then draw illustrations to represent each one. If you live in Wyoming and you put Yellowstone Park on your map, you can draw a buffalo at the location of Yellowstone Park, then also write in the name of the park. If you live in New York, you can draw the Statue of Liberty on your map and label it. It doesn't matter what you pick, but your illustration should represent the site in some way.

Find an image of your state capitol building and draw it on your map next to your state capital.

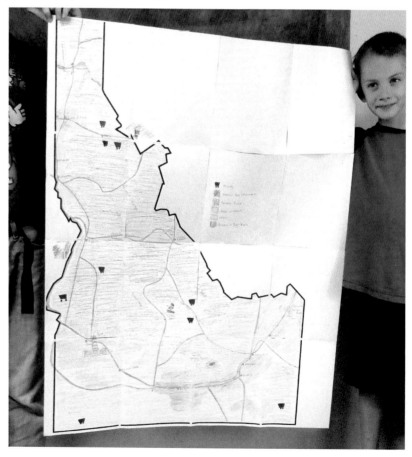

Once your illustrations are done, color them and then color the rest of your state according to landscape. Farmland should look like farmland, forests should look like forests, deserts should look like deserts, and so on. If there are named forests or other features, you can label those on your map as well.

☺ ☺ ☻ EXPLORATION: My State Capitol Building

Find your state capital on a map of your state. Draw your state capitol building on a sheet of paper. Cut it out and glue it in the middle of a sheet of card stock. Cut the card stock in half the long way, right through your drawing of your capitol building. Cut two long thin strips of paper from another sheet of card stock in a contrasting color. Fold these in half the long way. Coat them with glue inside the fold, and then use them to glue the cut-in-half picture of your capitol building to another sheet of card stock to make a folder. Draw and write information about your capitol building inside your folder. You could include the architects, history of the building, interesting features, what happens there, and so on.

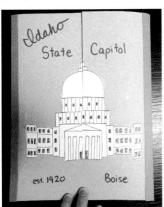
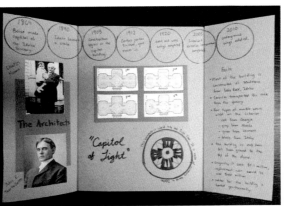

☺ ☺ ☻ EXPEDITION: Capitol Tour

Arrange to go on a tour of your state capitol building. Learn about the history of the building and other details before you go. Be prepared with one or two good questions for your guide. You may even be able to sit in on part of a legislative session or meet with one of your state's politicians if you schedule it ahead of time.

☻ EXPLORATION: Your State Has A Constitution

Look up and read your state's constitution. All fifty states have a constitution just for that state. Generally they're modeled after the United States Constitution, but they're often longer and more detailed. You can find yours at your local library or online.

☺ ☻ EXPLORATION: Local Affairs

Read or watch the local news every day for a week. Especially pay attention to politics and current events within your state. Pick

Fabulous Fact

Your state representative goes to your state capitol and works to make good things happen and works to protect the interests of his or her constituents in your district back home, but they can do a much better job if they know what is important to you, what kinds of challenges you're facing that government has an impact on, and what your opinion on current events is.

When you write your letter, don't just vent. Be clear and give good reasons for why you feel the way you do.

Additional Layer

County sheriffs are autonomous in most states. They don't answer to the governor, the local county, or the federal government. Their job is to uphold the law and protect the people of their county. That's why this is an elected position.

Find out more about your local sheriff. This person is a very important safeguard between you and criminals and between you and government officials.

one current issue that you think is important and write to your local state representative about the issue.

☺ ☺ EXPLORATION: My State Government

Make a poster showing the organization of your state government. Find pictures of your governor, lieutenant governor, state senator, state representative, county sheriff, county council, and city mayor, and place them on the poster in the correct places.

Not all of these positions will necessarily apply to you. Every state is set up a little differently. Also, you may not live within city limits, so you may not have a mayor, for example. Or your state may not have counties or sheriffs but instead have a Town Meeting. Adjust according to your local government.

☺ ☺ ☺ EXPEDITION: Attend A City Council Meeting

Attend a city council meeting, a town hall, or another local government meeting in your area. The dates, times, and locations should be posted on your city's website. You'll get to hear discussions about the local decisions being made and what is happening in your area.

☺ ☺ ☺ EXPEDITION: Community Organizations

Most communities have service organizations that meet and then go out and help fill a need in their communities. Find a service organization near you and ask if there's a project or day of community service you can get involved in.

Some local organizations you might try include the Lion's Club, Elk's Club, the local food bank, shelters, 4 -H groups, your library, Habitat for Humanity, your Chamber of Commerce, or other local organizations. Most nursing homes also have service opportunities. You can inquire at any of your local government offices or your library. You may also find contacts through your town, city, or county website.

Once in contact, get involved in a service opportunity they provide. When we get involved locally, we begin to feel pride and a connection with our local area and our home state.

☺ ☺ ☻ EXPLORATION: Economy

Find out which industries are important in your state. Is there manufacturing? Mining? Farming? Fishing? Tourism? Medicine? Financial Services? Is your state known for being the home of any important companies, industries, or products?

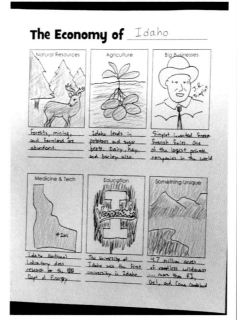

Make a list and then use that information to complete "The Economy of _____" printable from the end of this unit. Fill in the name of your state in the blank. In each box draw a picture representing each category of economic activity in your state. In the "Something Unique" box, find something your state does especially well, or something that is only in your state.

☺ ☺ ☻ EXPLORATION: Natural Resources

Find out what the major natural resources are in your state. Do you get a lot of tourism to your mountains or beaches? Do you have abundant timber or mining? Do you have fisheries or farmland? Do you have oil or mining?

Use the "_____ Natural Resources" printable from the end of this unit. Fill in the possessive form of your state's name in the blank. Then draw a picture on the puzzle showing some scenery from your state. The picture should include some of the major natural resources. If you live in Idaho you might have a picture

Additional Layer

This is a great time to do a map of the counties in your state as well. Just search for an outline map of counties in your state. Print it and label it.

Of course, if you live in Texas, you might want to rethink that. Texas has 254 counties! That's a lot of labeling.

Most states have regions as well. Look for maps of regions in your state and create your own regional map.

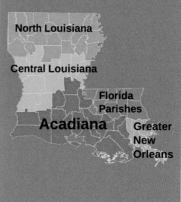

On the Web

You can find information about every state at Sheppard Software. http://www.sheppardsoftware.com/usaweb/snapshot/Alabama.htm.

For high schoolers we recommend the Wikipedia articles about each state.

Writer's Workshop

Make a crossword puzzle with words about your state. Write clues for each word. It's helpful to use graphing paper for your crossword puzzle so you can keep all the lines and boxes straight. When you're finished, see if someone can solve it.

Younger kids who can write words, but not clues, can make a state word search instead. Just write the words in on the squares of the graph paper, then fill in the remaining blanks with any letters from the alphabet.

Additional Layer

Find out some crazy laws about your state by looking online. In Arizona it's illegal for donkeys to sleep in bathtubs and in Georgia it's illegal to keep an ice cream cone in your back pocket on Sundays. Look up some weird laws from your state.

Additional Layer

Meet with someone who has lived in your state for a long time. Ask them about what life was like decades ago, what changes they've witnessed, and what stories they remember from the past.

of mountains with farmland in front. On each puzzle piece, corresponding to the picture, write one natural resource from your state. Then cut out the puzzle pieces and the title and glue them to another sheet of paper.

There are also three flaps to cut out and glue to your sheet of paper. Choose three natural resources from your state and write each one on the cover of a flap. Under the flap, write a sentence about the resource, how it is used, where exactly it can be found, how important it is, or some other fact.

☺ ☺ ☺ EXPEDITION: Meet The Helpers

Arrange for a tour of one of the government offices, the fire station, police station, or another local business that helps in your community. Talk with the people who work there. Find out what their jobs are and how they help in your community.

When we visited our fire station we got to dress like fire fighters, explore the trucks, squirt a fire hose, learn about fire safety, and see the areas fire fighters cook, exercise, and relax at the station. We also got to go through a smoke simulation where a full sized model of a house was dark and filled with artificial smoke from a fog machine and we practiced how to get out.

☺ ☺ ☺ EXPLORATION: Distribution Map

Create a distribution map of your state. Start with an outline map; all the state maps can be found at http://www.layers-of-learning. com/layers-of-learning-printables/.

Then choose what you want to show the distribution of. Here are some ideas: rainfall, population, climate, religion, race, income, or tree species. Research and create your map.

☺ ☺ ☻**EXPEDITION: Become A Tourist In Your Own Back Yard**

Approach where you live as a tourist would. Very often we live in a place for a long time, but miss out on neat opportunities because we aren't on vacation here. Look up some interesting things to do in your state. Search for neat museums, parks, attractions, landmarks, and nature areas. Go for a visit in your state like a tourist would and experience all it has to offer.

☺ ☺ ☻**EXPLORATION: Fun Facts Booklet**

Create a fun facts miniature booklet about your state. Look up 10 interesting facts about your state and write each one on a page in your mini book. Illustrate each page. You can make a mini book by cutting pages in half and then folding each half to create a quarter sheet sized pages. Add a card stock cover. Sew up the center to create a binding, or just staple along the center fold for a stapled binding.

☺ ☺ ☻**EXPLORATION: State Painting**

Make a colorful painting featuring your state. Start by finding a simple outline of your state map online. Print it and cut it out. Tape it down to a piece of canvas (we used prepared canvas from Walmart) or art paper with masking tape, pressing only lightly so it will come off when you've finished painting. Then choose a color palette and cover your whole canvas with paint. We used watercolors, but any kind of paint will do. Let it dry for an hour and then peel the state outline off, leaving a white space in the shape of your state. Let it dry completely.

On The Web

Learning Games for Kids has free flash games for every single state. You can learn or review state symbols, learn to spell state vocab words, put together a flag puzzle, and more.

http://www.learning-gamesforkids.com/us-state-games.html

Additional Layer

You can make really cool state string art using a piece of wood, small nails, a hammer, and some string. Draw an outline sketch of your state on your board. Pound small nails all of the way around the border. Tie off the string to one nail, and then begin wrapping it all over the interior of your state, looping around the nails in any pattern you like.

SCIENCE: HABITATS

On the Web

Play "Wild Kratts Habitats" from PBS Kids. http://pbskids.org/wildkratts/habitats/

Your player travels through different habitats and you learn a bit about animals that live in that habitat as you go along.

Additional Layer

In this unit we talk mostly about terrestrial habitats. Freshwater habitats include: marshes, streams, rivers, lakes, and estuaries. Marine habitats include: salt marshes, the coast, the intertidal zone, reefs, bays, the open sea, the sea bed, deep water, and submarine vents.

This pike lives in a lake habitat.

A habitat is the place where an animal or plant lives. It includes the landscape, like cliffs, valleys, lakes, seashore, and so on; the other animals; and the other plants in the location. It also includes things like the amount of rainfall, the average temperature, and the amount of light. A habitat can be very large, like the whole ocean if you're a blue whale, or very small, like the intestine of a dog if you're a parasitic worm.

There are a few major habitat zones. These include polar, mountain, seashore, ocean, rivers & lakes, wetlands, deserts, grasslands, tropical rainforests, temperate forests, and cities.

☺ ☻ EXPLORATION: Habitat Spinner

For this activity you'll need scissors, two pieces of card stock, a metal brad and crayons, markers, or colored pencils.

Cut two identical circles out of the two pieces of paper. The circles should fill up most of the page. To make our circles we traced around a dessert plate. Cut a triangular-shaped window in one circle. Place the other circle under the first, and trace the triangle opening with a pencil. Rotate the circle slightly and trace again, until you have made triangles all around the second circle.

Illustrate a different type of habitat inside each triangle. You should end up with five or six windows depending on how big you made your triangle opening. You will not have enough windows to write in every major type of habitat. That's okay, just choose your favorites. Label each of your habitat types. Fasten the two circles together with a brad in the center. Turn the window to view each of your habitats.

☺ EXPLORATION: Habitat Sort

At the end of this unit there are animal tiles. Cut them apart and cut apart the titles of the habitats. Glue the titles onto a separate piece of paper. Sort the animals into the correct habitat. If you would like, you can find background images online to print out to glue your animals to. The animals are on the printable in columns under their habitat. We tried to use familiar animals so your kids will be more likely to have some knowledge about where those animals live. You may want to do this activity after reading a few books about habitats.

☺ ☺ ☺ EXPLORATION: My Habitat

What habitat do you live in? Observe wildlife where you live for the next two weeks, or all through this unit. Write down sightings and what the animal was doing. Take note of plants and food sources as well. Tracks, knocked over garbage cans, droppings, and other animal signs should be noted too. Read up more on the animal or animals you spotted. Does it normally live where you spotted it? Did its behavior match what the book said?

☺ ☺ ☺ EXPEDITION: A Different Habitat

Visit a different habitat than the one your house is in. If you live in the city, you might take a trip to a nearby state park or seashore. If you live in a forest, maybe you can drive to a grassland or wetland. If you live in the desert you can visit a lake or the mountains. Pay close attention to the differences between the habitat where your house is and the habitat you visit. What are the differences in animals, plants, temperature, rainfall, and the landscape? How do you think those differences affect the types of plants and animals that live there?

Take photos that show the contrasts. In one area there may be pine trees and in another cacti. In one area there may be a river or stream and on the other a dry wash. Print your photos and arrange them on a poster board or sheets of paper. Put captions

Memorization Station

Write down these words and their definitions in your notebook and memorize their meanings.

- Habitat
- Niche
- Biotic
- Abiotic
- Sucession
- Biome

Additional Layer

Extremophiles are species that live in extreme habitats.

The bright blue color of this thermal pool in Yellowstone comes from bacteria that live in the hot water. Learn about hydrothermal vents, and bacteria that live deep underground as well.

On the Web

FileFolderFun.com has a free printable file folder habitat game. It's really more of a sorting activity.

http://filefolderfun.com/
SecondGradeScience/
AnimalHabitat

It's perfect for your younger kids.

Fabulous Fact

Urban environments are habitats for animals as well. Coyotes, raccoons, skunks, rats, pigeons, gulls, peregrines, swallows, and foxes all do well in cities and towns, not to mention all the bugs.

On the Web

Watch "Ecological Sucession" from Bozeman science: https://youtu.be/V49IovRSJDs.

Then watch TED talk "Glimpses of a Pristine Ocean" by Enric Sala. The first 3.5 minutes explain how a coral reef goes from dead to pristine. Note the species that signals a healthy coral reef. https://www.ted.com/talks/enric_sala/discussion.

Finally, watch "Pond Sucession" from Dr. Rudy Rosen: https://youtu.be/fYC5v5d0-jA.

Famous Folks

Henry Chandler Cowles studied ecological sucession in the Indiana Dunes near Lake Michigan.

below the photos explaining how photo #1 contrasts with photo #2, and so on.

☺ ☻ EXPLORATION: Diorama

Make a diorama of your favorite habitat. Put in pictures of authentic animals and plants. Paint a background scene of what the area really looks like. Which animals are predators and which are prey? Can you see a food web in your diorama?

☺ ☻ EXPLORATION: Ecological Succession

Ecological succession is the process of a habitat recovering from a disturbance over time. The disturbance could be natural like a volcanic explosion, a mudslide, a flood, or a wildfire. A disturbance could also be man-made like logging or clearing land for farming.

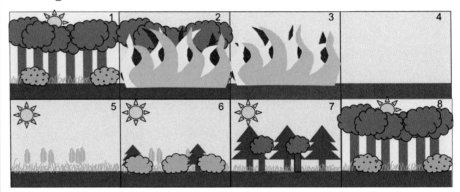

Image by Katelyn Murphy, CC by SA 3.0, Wikimedia

There are two types of succession: primary and secondary. Primary succession is when the land is completely barren, like after a volcanic explosion, a glacier, or a sand dune growing grasses for the first time. The first things to grow back are lichens, then grasses, then small plants and bushes, then trees, and finally a mature forest.

In secondary succession the soil is not completely destroyed. This would be after an event like a forest fire, a flood, or a drought. In this case the first species to recover are grasses and small plants, then small trees, and finally a mature forest. The first plants to come back after a disturbance are called "pioneers." The mature environment is called a climax community.

The time it takes to go from bare ground to a mature environment depends on the habitat. A redwood forest could take 500 years to grow back while a grassland may only take one year to recover.

Different plants and animals thrive at each of the stages of ecological succession as their habitat changes. Change in habitats is normal and constant. The changes can be big, like a massive windstorm that blows over thousands of acres of trees, or they can be small, like one tree that falls and opens the forest floor to sunlight.

Of course, the exact stages of ecological succession will depend on the environment where the disturbance happens. A desert's ecological succession will be very different from a forest or a grassland.

At the end of this unit is a notebooking page for succession. In the "Disturbances" chart, list types of disturbances that might clear land. In the "Types of Succession" chart, write the definitions for each type. Finally, there are two storyboards, one for a forest succession and one for a coral reef. Illustrate them to show how succession looks in those habitats.

☺ ☻ EXPLORATION: Organisms Need Four Things

Every living thing needs food, water, shelter, and space. It gets these from its habitat. Consider a date palm in an oasis in the Sahara Desert. Where does it get its food, water, shelter, and space? What about the white-winged guan that lives in the cloud forests of Bolivia? What does the wobbegong carpet shark of the coral reefs of Indonesia need to live? They all need the food, water, shelter, and space that their specific habitats give them.

Title a notebook page "Habitat." Beneath, write "All living things need food, water, shelter, and space." Draw four boxes that fill up the rest of your page. In each box draw a different animal in its habitat. Include all four things the animal needs. Choose animals from a variety of environments and do some research if you need to. Label the four things in your pictures each animal needs.

☺ ☻ EXPLORATION: Niche

A niche is the specific role a plant or animal plays in its habitat. It would include where the organism lives, what it eats, what eats it, how much space it requires, and so on. The niche is the one spot the organism occupies inside the web of interactions happening in the habitat.

Watch "Mangroves Swamps" from 5050 Community on YouTube: https://youtu.be/rolfvEnPnNA to learn about the roles of several different species in a mangrove swamp in South Africa.

Take notes as you watch. Write down the name of each species as the actors talk about it. Under the species, make a list of the things it does in its environment as well as ways it fits into the habitat it lives in. Illustrate your notes and put them in a notebook.

Additional Layer

In March of 2017 a cruise ship ran aground on a coral reef in the Raja Ampat Islands, Indonesia. 1600 square meters of reef was destroyed. It will have to start over with a new sucession. Marine biologists estimate it will take decades for the reef to recover.

Fabulous Fact

Some living things are pretty adaptable to a wide variety of environments. They are known as generalists.

Others have very specific requirements that might involve a specific food, a small temperature range, or the absence of a certain type of predators or competitors. These are called specialists.

Koalas eat only eucalyptus leaves and have a small range in Australia. Photo by Arnaud Gaillard, CC by SA 4.0.

Fabulous Facts

Watch "Ecological Niche" from Bozeman Science: https://youtu.be/z31y-ZtegZ8

Fabulous Fact

Different ecologists categorize biomes differently. There is no set standard defining which biomes exist and where precisely they are on earth. Some scientists name five biomes while others say there are twenty.

Also, biomes are very generalized. You can look at nearly any map of biomes and realize that it's not entirely accurate. You'll be aware that there's a desert or a temperate forest or even a tundra climate that is not shown on the map. But the concept of a biome is only useful if it is generalized.

On the Web

This site gives five biomes. But as you click on the links to read more about each biome, there are sub-biomes you can learn more about.

http://www.ucmp.berkeley.edu/glossary/gloss5/biome/

Fabulous Fact

Antarctica has a simple biome with few species.

☺ ☺ ☺ EXPLORATION: Biomes

A biome is a large ecological area on earth with plants and animals that require similar conditions. A biome is broader than a habitat and may include several habitats within it. For example, the rainforests of Africa are a biome, but the habitat of the okapi is only above 1,600 feet in elevation within the rainforest. So a biome is a geographical area that can be mapped for the whole globe, but a habitat is specific to every individual species.

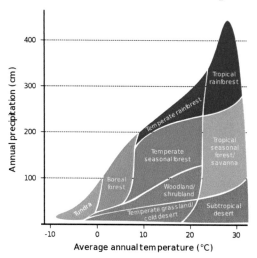

Biomes are dependent on the amount of rainfall, combined with the average yearly temperature. This graphic shows how biomes depend on the climate.

At the end of this unit is a simplified biome map of the world. It does not include aquatic biomes. Color by number.

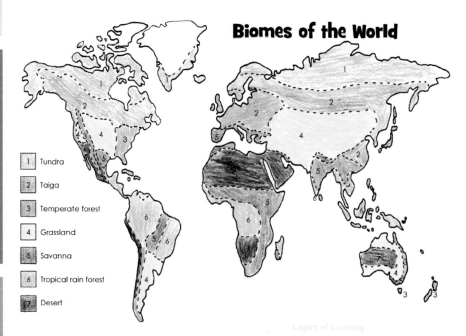

Biomes of the World

1 Tundra
2 Taiga
3 Temperate forest
4 Grassland
5 Savanna
6 Tropical rain forest
7 Desert

☺ ☺ ☺ EXPLORATION: Ecological Levels of Organization

We can organize ecological levels of life. The first level is the organism or individual. The second level is the population, or all of the individuals of a particular species in a particular place. The third level is the community, or all the living organisms in a particular place that interact with one another. The fourth level is the ecosystem, including the living and non-living things in a particular place. The fifth level is the biome, a large geographical area with a similar climate. And the sixth level is the biosphere, the living layer of the entire earth.

Make a series of concentric circles to show the levels of ecological organization. We used a mathematical compass to make our circles. Here are the radius measurements we used:

4.25 in (10.5 cm)
3.5 in (9 cm)
3 in (7.5 cm)
2.25 in (5.5 cm)
1.5 in (4 cm)
1 in (2.5 cm)

Then we punched a hole in the top of each circle and fastened them together with a ball chain key chain. You could also use a metal brad or a piece of string or yarn to fasten the circles together. We liked how the bright colors the papers we chose turned out, but you could use any color or just white paper.

Finally, write the levels of organization starting with "organism" on the smallest circle. Choose an animal to be your focus. We chose the gray wolf. We drew the gray wolf alone, in a population of gray wolves, in a community with other plants and animals, in an ecosystem with living and non-living things, and then we drew the gray wolf's biome. On the final circle we drew the planet.

Additional Layer

The organization of life begins with the cell, the smallest unit of life and extends up to the biosphere. But the top six levels are considered the levels of ecology. You can learn or review all of the levels by labeling foam cups with the level names and gluing pictures representing each level to the cups.

Mix them up and have the kids put them back in order for a quick quiz.

Additional Layer

If you change one element on any of the ecological levels, you can have drastic changes to the whole system. A good example of this are the wolves of Yellowstone National Park. They were eradicated in the early 20th century and then reintroduced in 1995. Detailed studies have been done to show the far reaching effect this one species has on the whole ecosystem of Yellowstone. Look up more information.

THE ARTS: ARCHITECTURE

Expedition

Plan an architectural expedition. Many government buildings and churches are open to the public for tours. If possible, arrange to meet with someone who can tell you of the building's history and architectural style. Take a look at this article about a tour of the Washington State Capitol Building to get a feel for the kinds of details you are looking for on your tour.

https://layers-of-learning.com/take-an-architectural-tour/

On The Web

This video, "Introduction to Architecture" by Stephanie Kvamme, would be a perfect introduction to architecture. Plan to watch it with your kids the first day of the unit as a jumping off place for learning about all of these famous buildings. It discusses why we have buildings and the history of architecture. It also has interesting facts about building codes, landscape design, and what architects do.

https://youtu.be/6Q8P-BcF-470

We are going to learn about some of the most beautiful and famous architectural structures on the earth during this unit. Just like art, the style of architecture changes over time and varies from place to place. During some historical periods, ornamentation and detail were highly favored. At other times, clean lines and functionalism over decoration was preferred. The materials used often depended on the climates of each location. Rather than trying to learn about every architectural style and movement over the course of the history of people building things over the entire earth, we will instead explore some of the most famous buildings and structures that you should know about. We will also learn the names for some of the architectural details and styles as we look at the buildings in each exploration.

Firmness, commodity, and delight were the requirements that Sir Henry Wotton said architecture needed. Firmness referred to the actual soundness of the structure and the way it was built. By commodity, he meant its usefulness. Buildings need to be well laid out and functional for their purposes. Finally, he maintained that buildings should be delightful, or in other words, beautiful and interesting to look at.

There are many recognizable buildings that dot the globe. This building is where the Houses of Parliament meet at Westminster, England. Photo by Tony Moorey, shared under CC license 2.0.

☺ ☺ ☺ **EXPLORATION: The Pyramids of Giza**
Egypt is the home of some of the huge pyramid-shaped tombs that were built in ancient days and are still standing today. The outside is impressive, but in addition, the pyramids have cham-

Famous Folks

Pericles, an Athenian statesman from the 5th century, brought architecture to its highest point in his day.

bers, tunnels, and galleries. Most of the interior hasn't been explored and is still a mystery to us. You can see a neat virtual tour of the pyramids and some of the interior chambers we have seen though. Go tour these amazing feats of architecture on the PBS website at http://www.pbs.org/wgbh/nova/pyramid/explore/.

☺ ☺ ☺ **EXPLORATION: The Parthenon**

The Parthenon was a building made in ancient times by the Greeks. It was a temple that was built for the Greek goddess, Athena. Over the years it served as a treasury, a Christian church, and a mosque. It has had a huge influence on Western architecture and hundreds of buildings have been modeled after parts of it, including many of the capitol buildings in the United States, libraries, and universities. The columns are an especially recog-

Additional Layer

To become an architect most people go to college for at least 4 years, usually 5-7. They earn a degree in architecture. Next, they get over 5,000 hours of on-the-job experience while working under the supervision of a licensed architect. Finally, they take an exam in order to become licensed. They have to know the building codes and laws, plus have an understanding of engineering and safety as well as beautiful design.

This painting shows what the Parthenon may have looked like, sitting atop the acropolis in Athens. It sat higher than the other buildings of the city.

Fabulous Fact

As you look at the amazing buildings during this unit, remember that most of them were built without electricity, power tools, vehicles, or modern technology.

Additional Layer

Choose one of these interesting buildings to create a poster about.

The Eiffel Tower

Chrysler Building

One World Trade Center

Big Ben

Lotus Temple

Space Needle

Forbidden City

Buckingham Palace

Arc de Triomphe

White House

Angkor Wat

Beijing National Stadium

Great Mosque of Djenne

Church of St. George

Machu Picchu

Pyramid of the Sun

Additional Layer

The Alhambra is a palace in Spain. It evolved over several centuries, with parts being added on as needed. There's a board game where you build your own Alhambra that would be fun to play during this unit.

nizable feature. Watch "Parthenon (Acropolis)" by Smarthistory to hear a terrific explanation of the ancient temple and learn about its details: https://youtu.be/tWDflkBZC6U.

Build your own columned building using card stock and empty toilet paper tubes as your columns. Look up the names of various column styles and pattern yours after one of the styles.

☺ ☺ ☻ EXPLORATION: Domes

Filippo Brunelleschi lived in Italy during the Renaissance. He used geometry to create beautiful buildings. He was an architect, engineer, and an artist. He designed the Florence Cathedral, with the largest brick dome in the world. We can see domes on many buildings today. Have you ever seen one? What kind of a building was it on?

The Florence Cathedral, photo by Bruce Stokes, CC 2.0 license

Domes are the upper half of a sphere, also called a hemisphere, on the roof line of a building. They have been built all over the world over many centuries, going all the way back to the time of the Mesopotamians. They are most often seen on government buildings, churches, and sports stadiums.

They are constructed in many different ways, but today we are going to build a geodesic dome made of plastic straws. Geodesic domes use triangles to create the domes, and are very strong because of the many triangular shapes that distribute the weight of the dome. You'll need lots of plastic straws in two colors, brads, a small hole punch (about 1/16" diameter punch), a ruler, and some scissors.

The two colors of straws help us keep track of the different lengths. Cut 35 pieces of one color that are 5 1/2" long. Cut 30 pieces of your second color that are 4 3/4" long. Hole punch the ends of each straw. You'll be using brads to connect the ends of the straws. Begin by making a circle using ten longer straws, and adding triangles of alternating colors at each connection.

Now attach a green upright coming out from the top of each green triangle, then connect the green uprights to form pentagons (5-sided shapes). Add inside supports to each pentagon using the shorter, yellow straws. At this point you should have 5 green pentagons, each with yellow interior support beams.

Finally, add another horizontal row of the shorter, yellow straws, connecting the tops of your green pentagons in a yellow pentagon. Finally, add interior support beams on your top pentagon with the shorter, yellow straws, making each one meet in the center at a final connection point. Your geodesic dome is complete!

☺ ☺ ☻ EXPLORATION: The Colosseum

The Colosseum in Rome, Italy is the largest amphitheater in the entire world. Its history is really fascinating and a little gruesome too. It held up to 80,000 spectators, who all came to see plays, animal hunts, battles, gladiator fights, and more. Watch "Ancient Colosseum: A Virtual Reality Experience With Oculus Rift" by Radical Impact, to see a virtual reality look at what it would've been like to be in the Colosseum in its heyday, while listening to a

Writer's Workshop

What kind of a house would you live in if you could live anywhere you wanted? Design your dream house in a drawing, then write about it. When I was young I dreamed of living in an underground hobbit hole.

Memorization Station

Learn these words and what they mean, then keep an eye out for them as you're looking at famous architecture.

Column

Cupola

Portico

Buttress

Obelisk

Finial

Blueprint

Arch

Dome

Rose Window

Tower

Stained glass

Spire

Turret

Memorization Station

Vitruvius, a Roman architect, described the three principles of a good building:

1. Durability - stand up over many years and be sound and well-constructed

2. Utility - be useful and fulfill its intended purpose

3. Beauty - be lovely to look at and artistic

Memorize those three principles. As you learn about each of the buildings in this unit, test them against his three criteria.

Famous Folks

Here are some famous architects to learn about:

Frank Lloyd Wright
Frank Gehry
Zaha Hadid
Le Corbusier
Ludwig Mies van der Rohe
Philip Johnson
Christopher Wren
Michelangelo
Andrea Palladio
Julia Morgan
Shigeru Ban
Frederick Law Olmsted
Filippo Brunelleschi
Edwin Lutyens
Adolf Loos
William Le Baron Jenney
Maya Lin

narration about its history and architecture as you see the action: https://youtu.be/bAWTJO6oz-o.

This is the Colosseum. It is also called the Flavian Amphitheatre after the Flavian Dynasty, the three emperors who reigned during its construction. Photo by Jerzy Strzelecki and shared under CC 3.0 license.

☺ ☺ ☺ EXPLORATION: The Pantheon

The Pantheon is a circular building with a large portico, or porch, that is surrounded by columns. It was built by the ancient Romans as a temple. It has been used throughout the ages and is still in use today in Italy. Now it is a museum that showcases its beautiful architecture.

Use the "Label The Pantheon" printable to learn some architectural terms. Read the definitions for each of the terms, then try to identify that part on the Pantheon diagram. Cut out the archi-

Here is a view of the Pantheon's beautiful interior. Photo courtesy of Stefan Bauer under CC 2.5 license.

tectural terms from the bottom of the worksheet and glue them to the correct places on the diagram.

Column: an upright pillar that is typically a cylinder shape that provides support to a building

Portico: a covered porch attached to a building that has a roof supported by columns

Pediment: the triangle-shaped section at the top of a portico

Stepped dome: a dome that has beveled edges, or steps, as it goes upward instead of being smooth.

Oculus: a round, circular window in the center of a dome.

Drum: a circular wall that supports a dome.

Coffered Ceiling: a patterned wall overhead, made up of sunken panels

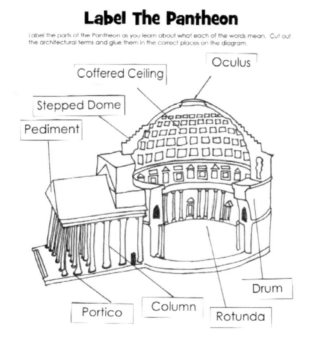

Label The Pantheon

Label the parts of the Pantheon as you learn about what each of the words mean. Cut out the architectural terms and glue them in the correct places on the diagram.

Coffered Ceiling · Oculus · Stepped Dome · Pediment · Portico · Column · Rotunda · Drum

On The Web

Watch this Khan Academy lecture about the Hagia Sophia with breathtaking views of the amazing church.

https://www.khanacademy.org/humanities/ap-art-history/early-europe-and-colonial-americas/medieval-europe-islamic-world/v/hagia-sophia-istanbul

Expedition

Go out and about and search for each of the architectural elements on the "Architecture Scavenger Hunt" printable. Cross out each item as you find it.

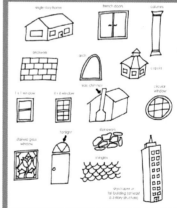

Older kids can also learn and search for various home styles - Victorian, Craftsman, Townhouse, Bungalow, Art Deco, Colonial, Log Home, Mediterranean, Modern, Ranch, and Neoclassical are good ones to start with.

☺ ☺ ☺ **EXPLORATION: The Pisa Cathedral and its Leaning Tower**

The Duomo di Pisa, or Pisa Cathedral, is a lovely church in Pisa, Italy. In 1772, the people of the church decided to build a bell tower for the church. As it was being built, the tower began to lean! They kept building anyway, despite the soft ground below the foundation of the tall tower. Architects and engineers work to secure the tower now, so it doesn't fall over. They leave it leaning though, since that is what has made the tower so famous in the first place.

In your sketchbook, draw some other famous buildings and what they would look like if they were leaning like the Leaning Tower of Pisa. What would your house look like if it were leaning? Write a journal entry about what you would have done if you were the architect of the Leaning Tower of Pisa. Would you have fixed the foundation right away? Would you leave it leaning? On the one

Additional Layer
Learn the story of Quasimodo, the Hunchback of Notre Dame.

Additional Layer
There are churches and cathedrals all over the world with various styles of architecture. The first is a Buddhist temple in Tasmania. The second is a Christian church is China. The third is a cathedral in Australia.

hand, the bad foundation was a mistake, but on the other hand, we probably wouldn't be talking about this bell tower at all without its famous lean.

The Pisa Baptistry is shown in the foreground, the Pisa Cathedral in the middle ground, and the Tower of Pisa in the background. Photo by Florian Hirzinger, shared via Wikimedia Commons under CC 4.0 license.

☺ ☺ ☺ EXPLORATION: Notre Dame
Watch "The History of France's Notre Dame Cathedral" by CBS to learn all about this famous Cathedral in Paris, France. Take illustrated notes using the Cathedral of Notre Dame printable as you watch. In each of the four circles on the printable, draw an architectural detail you see from the video. You'll draw things like the huge bells, gargoyles, statues, buttresses, flying buttresses, stained glass windows, or other ornamentation you see. Then include captions with interesting information about the cathedral and the details you chose to draw. https://youtu.be/5ux4LC1kd-QI

☺ ☺ ☺ EXPLORATION: Comparing Two Cathedrals
A cathedral is a Christian church that contains the seat of a bishop. It is the principle church within a diocese, or district of the church. Cathedrals are often fancy, ornate buildings and are meant as a place of reverence and spirituality. Many cathedrals have symbolic artwork and statues that tell about the life and teachings of Jesus Christ.

Although cathedrals have these things in common, they also differ. We'll look at two cathedrals and try to spot some differences. Research St. Basil's Cathedral and the Cologne Cathedral online. Make a list of at least 10 differences between the two cathedrals.

St. Basil's Cathedral was begun in 1555 as a memorial to the great Russian victory over the Tartars. Tsar Ivan IV had it built overlooking Moscow's Red Square. It is an eclectic structure, borrowing from many different styles. At first glance you notice the many-tiered domes that were built after the timber churches of northern Russia. The brickwork is more like that seen in the southern regions of Russia. And you can also spot many European Renaissance influences. It is currently used as a museum, but no longer serves as an active church. Watch this footage, "Saint Basil Cathedral in Moscow, Russia, 2012" by Julian Kang: https://youtu.be/thyFSZ6a7gg.

The Cathedral at Cologne is in Germany. Its construction was begun in 1248, but not completely finished until 1880, over 600 years later. It has tall spires and intricate stonework. Stained glass windows, buttresses, and pinnacles adorn the building, and archways, fresco paintings, and statues fill the interior. It is still used as a church and holds regular services, but visitors can also go in and visit to see the beautiful cathedral. "Cologne Cathedral, Germany" by WorldSiteGuides provides a great tour: https://youtu.be/GgRMY6dKCyU.

Look at each of these cathedrals and compare the two. Draw a simple sketch of each one in your sketchbook, St. Basil's with its colorful onion domes and the Cologne Cathedral with its tall spires. In between the two sketches write the things they have in common. On the outsides, write the differences you see between the two cathedrals.

St. Basil's Cathedral. Photo by A. Savin and shared under CC 3.0 license.

The Cologne Cathedral. Photo by Karen Loutzenhiser.

Additional Layer

St. Peter's Basilica is a famous church in Italy. Technically, it is not a cathedral because it is not the church of a bishop. It was one of the most ambitious of the 16th century building projects though. Bramante, Raphael, Michelangelo, and Bernini all contributed.

Additional Layer

Many of these famous buildings are under constant restoration. Look closely at the photograph of the Cologne Cathedral and you will see the scaffolding on the left spire. People are constantly working to maintain the buildings to preserve their history and architecture. The art, windows, and stonework of the Cologne Cathedral are constantly being restored. This is the small workshop at the cathedral where they are trying to preserve the history of the old building.

Writer's Workshop

There are amazing castles dotting the globe. For some inspiration, watch "Top 10 Most Amazing Castles and Palaces Ever Built" by Be Amazed: https://youtu.be/AM-h8uVETYAI

Now imagine an adventure story that takes place in a castle. Put yourself in the story as one of the characters. Describe your bedroom in the castle. Who are your friends? What do you do all day? Write the story of an adventure that you and your friends have in the castle.

Fabulous Fact

Modern architects consider more than just the building they are designing by itself. They look at the surrounding areas. Often they even consider things like how their building will change the city skyline. Modern cities often have skylines full of skyscrapers. This is the city of Hong Kong with its many skyscrapers.

☺ ☺ ☺ EXPLORATION: The Taj Mahal

The Taj Mahal is a marble mausoleum, a building to house the dead. Shah Jahan, a Mogul emperor, built it in memory of his beloved wife, Mumtaz Mahal. It is a geometrically perfect building, creating a unifying and symmetrical effect. The entire building is symmetrical. Its reflection in the nearby pool on the grounds also creates a line of symmetry. The gardens surrounding it have symmetrical plantings and pathways. The tile work, arches, and hallways inside are all symmetrical as well.

Use graphing paper to design your own perfectly symmetrical building. First, draw a line down the center of your paper, directly on the center grid line. You can make the building look however you wish, but whatever you draw on one side of the line, you must mirror on the other side of the line to create a symmetrical building.

☺ ☺ EXPLORATION: Form Follows Function

Louis Sullivan, an American architect, observed that, "form follows function." He was searching for ways to make buildings more functional instead of just building things the way it had always been done before. After considering what was needed in cities, he developed tall, steel skyscrapers. Just think of how much use, or function, there is in a skyscraper. They serve many people of a city well, with a very small physical footprint on the ground. The idea that the form of a building should be the primary determinant of what it looks like is a modern one. Decoration, beauty, and tradition had been the standard before, but Sullivan recognized a new need in the modern world - function.

Use a set of wooden blocks to build a tall skyscraper. See how tall you can get it before it falls down. As you build, discuss how modern buildings and homes are different than buildings throughout other times and eras in the world.

☺ ☺ ☺ EXPLORATION: The Tallest Buildings

The Empire State Building in New York City was the world's tallest building when it was built, but now it isn't even in the top ten. Buildings just keep getting taller and taller. Look up the tallest buildings in the world currently. Make a quick sketch of each building and its height in your sketchbook.

☺ ☺ ☺ **EXPLORATION: Sydney Opera House**

The Sydney Opera House sits right near Sydney Harbor. Jorn Utzon was the architect who created the recognizable building after his design was chosen out of a contest of architects. His design features a roof that looks like sails. Sometimes projectors are used to make the sails light up. Watch"Sydney Opera House: Lighting the Sails - The Spinifex Group - Vivid LIVE 2013" by Sydney Opera House to see how the sails light up with colorful projections: https://youtu.be/vZljVZ1vc4c.

Sydney Opera House

Make your own Sydney Opera House by cutting out crescent shapes from white paper plates. Cut one end off of each crescent where the sail is in contact with the ground. Paint the harbor. You can leave the sails white, or you can color them like the colorful projections.

Additional Layer

Pearl Tower in Shanghai, China is an interesting combination of form and function. It's a TV and radio tower. Rather than just put an ugly tower up though, it was designed with colorful spheres and observatory levels. Inside is a restaurant, a shopping center, and a hotel.

Coming up next . . .
Unit 4-20
Terrorism
America in Review
Conservation
Creative Kids

My ideas for this unit:

Title: _____ **Topic:** _____

_____

_____

_____

_____

_____

_____

_____

_____

_____

_____

Title: _____ **Topic:** _____

_____

_____

_____

_____

_____

_____

_____

_____

_____

_____

_____

Title: _____ **Topic:** _____

_____

_____

_____

_____

_____

_____

_____

_____

_____

_____

Title: _____ **Topic:** _____

_____
_____
_____
_____
_____
_____
_____
_____
_____
_____

Title: _____ **Topic:** _____

_____
_____
_____
_____
_____
_____
_____
_____
_____
_____

Title: _____ **Topic:** _____

_____
_____
_____
_____
_____
_____
_____
_____
_____
_____

Invention of the Airplane

The airplane was one of the first of the new inventions of the technology age, the time when rapid inventions changed the way people did just about everything.

Wilbur and Orville Wright, two brothers from Ohio, invented a way to get a fixed wing aircraft to stay in the air and to control it while it was up there. They made their first successful flight in 1903. They kept working on their plane design, making it better and better. By 1914 the airplane was being used in everyday life.

Technology Timeline

1903	**1907**	**1909**	**1910s**
Wilbur & Orville Wright invent the airplane	The first synthetic plastic, Bakelite, is invented	Synthetic fertilizer invented by Fritz Haber	Henry Ford creates the assembly line and interchangeable parts.

1928	**1930**	**1935**	**1937**
Penicillin discovered by Alexander Fleming	Over 70% of households in the U.S. electrified and all factories were driven by electricity.	Electron microscope invented; scientists see inside cells	Automatic washing machine invented; dozens of household appliances follow

1958	**1990**		
Integrated circuit, which makes modern computer technology possible, is invented	The World Wide Web and online language of HTML is created by Tim Berners-Lee		

8 Ways We Use _____

The Black Box

The Economy of _____

Natural Resources	Agriculture	Big Businesses

_____
_____
_____
_____

Medicine & Tech	Education	Something Unique

_____
_____
_____
_____

_____ Natural Resources

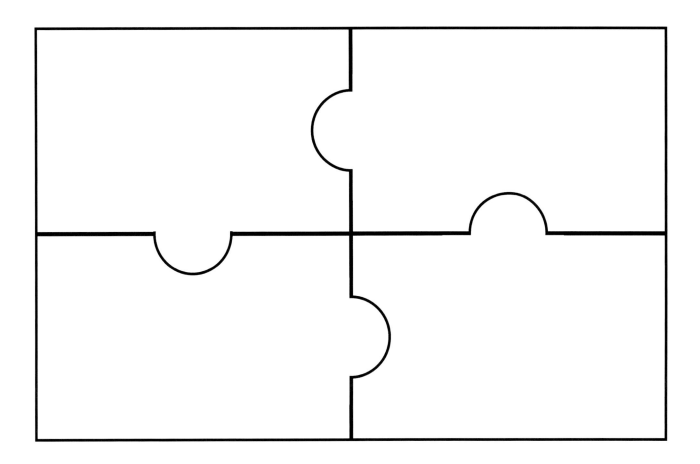

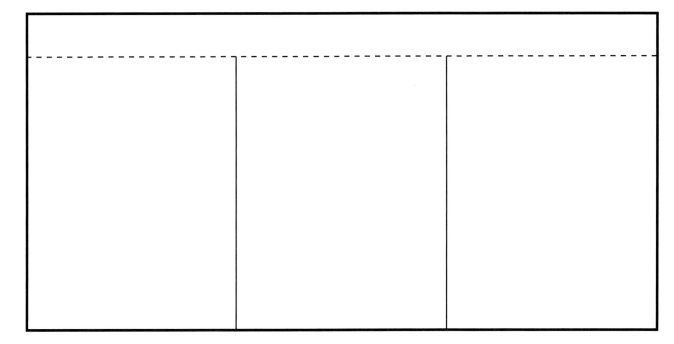

Jungle	Savanna	Forest

Arctic	Australian	Ocean

Ecological Succession

Disturbances	
natural	man-made

Types of Succession	
primary	secondary

bare land	pioneer species	fast growing trees	mature forest

bare rocks	pioneer species	small fishes	mature coral reef

Biomes of the World

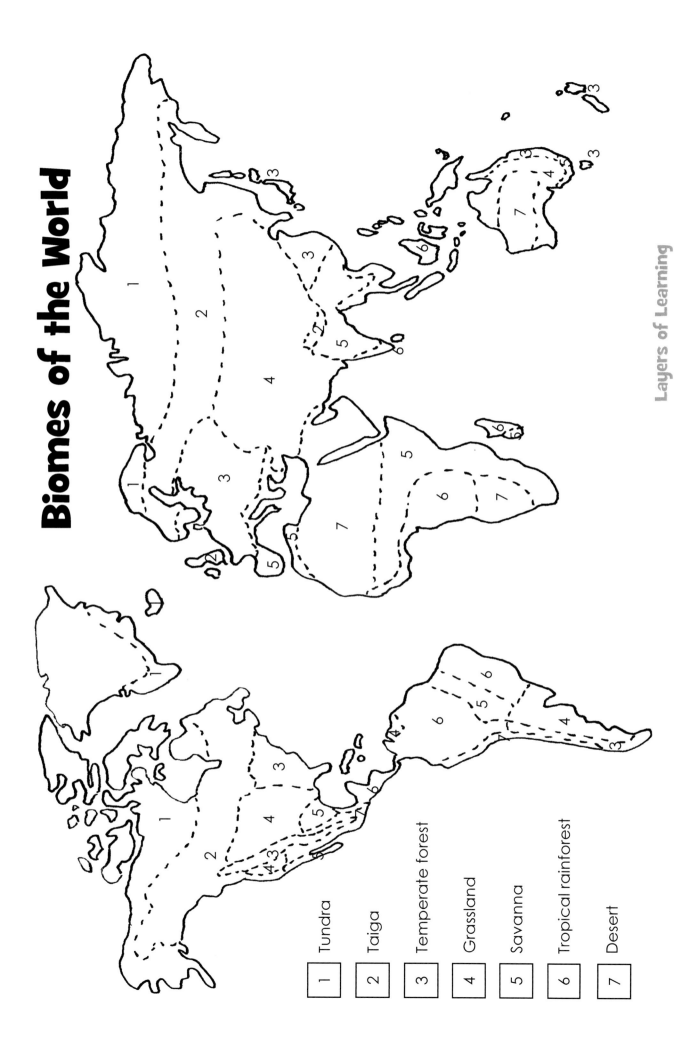

Layers of Learning

1	Tundra
2	Taiga
3	Temperate forest
4	Grassland
5	Savanna
6	Tropical rainforest
7	Desert

Label The Pantheon

Label the parts of the Pantheon as you learn about what each word means. Cut out the architectural terms and glue them in the correct places on the diagram.

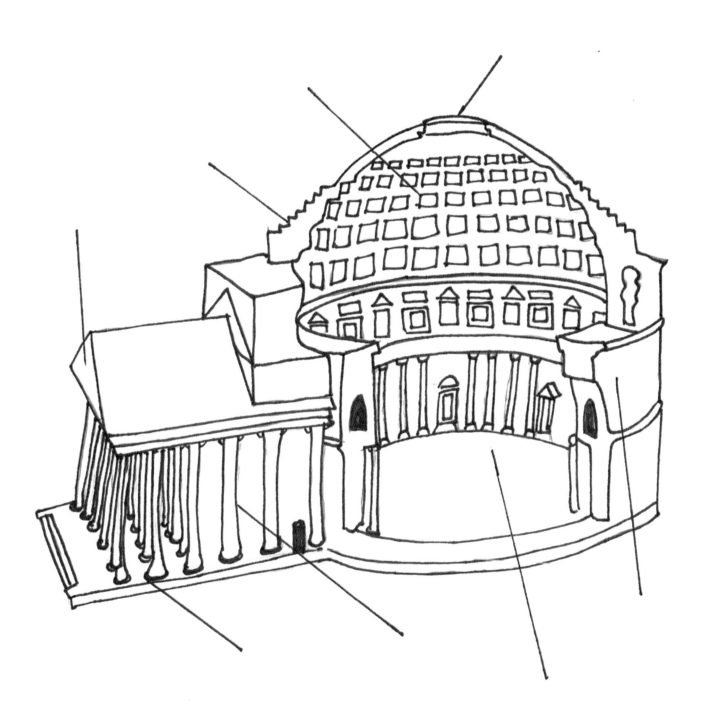

Coffered Ceiling	Oculus	Portico	Column
Stepped Dome	Drum	Rotunda	Pediment

The Cathedral of Notre Dame

Architecture Scavenger Hunt

single story home

french doors

columns

brickwork

arch

cupola

side chimney

circular window

1 x 1 window

4 x 4 window

stained glass window

fanlight

stonework

shingles

skyscraper or tall building (at least a 3 story structure)

About the Authors

Karen & Michelle . . .
Mothers, sisters, teachers, women who are passionate
about educating kids.
We are dedicated to lifelong learning.

Karen, a mother of four, who has homeschooled her kids for more than eight years with her husband, Bob, has a bachelor's degree in child development with an emphasis in education. She lives in Idaho, gardens, teaches piano, and plays an excruciating number of board games with her kids. Karen is our resident arts expert and English guru {most necessary as Michelle regularly and carelessly mangles the English language and occasionally steps over the bounds of polite society}.

Michelle and her husband, Cameron, have homeschooled their six boys for more than a decade. Michelle earned a bachelors in biology, making her the resident science expert, though she is mocked by her friends for being the Botanist with the Black Thumb of Death. She also is the go-to for history and government. She believes in staying up late, hot chocolate, and a no whining policy. We both pitch in on geography, in case you were wondering.

Visit our constantly updated blog for tons of free ideas,
free printables, and more cool stuff for sale:
www.Layers-of-Learning.com

Made in the USA
Middletown, DE
04 April 2025